CHILLERS 4

The New Man

Looking for Billy

by Iris Howden

Published in association with the Adult Literacy
and Basic Skills Unit

Hodder & Stoughton
LONDON SYDNEY AUCKLAND TORONTO

The publishers and ALBSU wish to acknowledge the contribution of the NEWMAT
Project, Nottinghamshire Local Education Authority, and of the Project Leader,
Peter Beynon, in the conception, writing and publication of the *Chillers* series.

British Library Cataloguing in Publication Data
Howden, Iris
    The new man. Looking for Billy.–(Chillers: 4).
    1. English language – Readers
    I. Title   II. National Institute of Adult Education (England and Wales), *Adult
    Literacy and Basic Skills Unit*   III. Series
    428.6

    ISBN 0 340 52105 8

First published 1989

Typeset by Gecko Ltd, Bicester, Oxon
Printed for the educational publishing division of Hodder and Stoughton Ltd,
Mill Road, Dunton Green, Sevenoaks, Kent by St Edmundsbury Press Ltd,
Bury St Edmunds, Suffolk

The New Man

The good-looking man stood behind his wife
at the grave.
He watched her place flowers on the grave,
saw her wipe a tear from her eye.
He read the name on the headstone.

> BRIAN TURNER
>
> Born 7th April 1952
> Died 10th July 1984

It was his own name,
his date of birth,
the day of his death.
The man hid a smile
as he led his wife back to the car.
She knew how to put on a good show.
She still put flowers on his grave – once a year.
'Rest in peace, Brian Turner,' he said softly.

He called himself Mark now.
He thought back to that night,
the night he'd died – or so everyone thought.
How he had fought for his life in the blaze
that had burnt his factory to the ground!
He'd often asked himself
whose body had been found in the ashes.
Was it some old tramp
who'd crept in out of the cold?
No one would ever know for sure.

Of course it had been her idea
to set up the fire –
to stage an accident,
so they could collect the insurance money.
What she hadn't told him
was that he'd be locked in his office,
that his death was part of the plan.
Well, she'd made a packet out of it.
Now it was her turn to pay.
He'd waited so long to get even.
Jumping through that window
had left more scars than those on his face –
scars deep inside – they took longer to heal.

Mark looked at himself in the driving mirror.
The plastic surgeon had done a good job.
In fact, he was much better-looking these days.
He'd got rid of his glasses and wore contact lenses.
He'd lost weight in the years he'd spent working
in the Middle East –
years in which he'd worked all hours.
He'd saved for the day
when he could come back
and settle his account with Diana.
It had been worth waiting for.

She'd played right into his hands
putting that advert in the paper:

**LONELY WIDOW WISHES TO MEET GENTLEMAN
WITH VIEW TO FRIENDSHIP, TRAVEL, ETC.**

She'd been taken in by the photo he'd sent.
He looked well –
a handsome man with his sun tan,
his new clothes,
his expensive car.
Soon they'd been dating.
Now after three months they were man and wife.
Again! And still she didn't suspect a thing.

He smiled as he swung the Jag
into the drive-way of their luxury house.
You had to say one thing for her –
she had taste,
she knew how to spend his money.
But this time, he'd be the one to collect.
He had a plan worked out.
Diana wasn't much of a driver.
She was always having some scrape or other
in her car.
What could be more natural than a car crash?
He would need help, of course.
He couldn't afford to be mixed up
with any funny business,
not after the big insurance policy
they'd both taken out.
'Just to be on the safe side,' she'd said.
'You never know what's going to happen.'

How true in your case, he thought.
That was another reason for getting in first.
Maybe she was planning another little 'accident'.
He rang his brother, Jimmy,
who'd helped him get out of the country
after the fire.
Jimmy wouldn't give him away –
he knew too much. He could trust Jimmy.

'We're going out with friends tomorrow,'
he told Jimmy.
'They're due to pick us up at 12.30
so you should have plenty of time.
Fix her brake pipes,
but make sure it looks like an accident.
We can't afford to have anything go wrong.'

***

After the crash the police came round to the house.
The older P.C. rang the bell.
'This is one part of the job I hate,' he said,
'bringing bad news.'

Two hours later Diana poured Jimmy
another drink.
'Here's to us,' she said.
'You're a clever boy. Two husbands
for the price of one.
Two lots of insurance money. Two perfect plans.'
She raised her glass.
'To the new man in my life,' she said.

Looking for Billy

On the train

I took the train south as soon as I could.
It took me a few days.
I had to buy some new clothes,
get a hair cut,
cadge a few quid from that brother of mine.
The way I saw it he owed it to me.
I'd kept quiet all those years
about his part in the robbery.
I'd done the time –
he could pay for it.

Now I had to find Sheila.
I had the address from her last letter –
not that she'd written often.
Sheila was never much of a letter writer.
Still she'd said all she had to say in a few words –
a real 'Dear John' it was.
She'd taken the kid and gone,
left Glasgow and gone back home to her mother –
or so she said.
I had my doubts.
Sheila was never one to let the grass grow
under her feet.
Well, some other mug would be keeping her now.

But the kid –
that was different –
he was my son.
It broke my heart to leave Billy.
I thought about him all the time
during those long years inside.
The last time I saw him he'd be about eleven –
dressed in his football kit,
the muddy ball pressed to his chest.
His fair hair was standing on end –
I never could make that bit at the back lie flat.
He'd just come from the park
as the police came to get me.
I'll never forget the look on his face
as they drove me away.
It will stay in my mind for ever.

Now, as the train sped over the border,
I took out the last photo I'd had from her –
the last time I heard from that bitch.
He was older, of course,
but somehow still the same –
the same spiky blonde hair,
the same look of hurt on his face,
the look I'd put there.
Well, now I was out.
I would try my best to make it up to him.
But first I had to find him.

The train was due into Nottingham at tea time.
I'd have to hurry –
find some cheap digs before dark.
Tomorrow I'd begin my search,
start looking for Billy.

The Flat

The next day I took a bus
to an estate east of the city.
I soon found the block of flats where she lived.
You couldn't miss it –
a high-rise tower in the middle of nowhere.
The kids had been busy with their spray cans –
pop groups, punk slogans, four-letter words.

The lift was out of order.
As I trudged up the seven flights of stairs,
I thought, 'You've come down in the world, girl.
You used to like the good life.'

Then she came to the door.
She'd lost her looks and had run to fat.
Her hair was dyed and dragged back in a ponytail.
When she saw me she nearly passed out.
Then she asked me in.
But there was no welcome in her voice.

A bloke sat at the table
with a newspaper and a mug of tea in front of him.
Two little kids played on the floor.
The room was scruffy and not very clean.
The furniture was cheap and tatty.
She said something to the bloke; he got up and left,
but not before he'd held out his hand
for a fiver from her purse.

'I'm sorry about the mess,' she said.
'If I'd known you were coming . . .
When did you get out?'
'Cut the small talk,' I said.
'I only want to know one thing.
Where's Billy? Tell me where he is.
Has he got a job?
Maybe I can see him at work.'

The Hostel

Half an hour later I was heading for the local nick.
I was feeling mad,
mad with Sheila for letting the lad run wild,
mad with myself for not being there
to keep him out of trouble.
Billy had been sent down for twelve months.
I had a job making them believe I was his dad.
Then I showed them Sheila's letter
and the photo of Billy.

One of the screws gave me an address – a hostel.
Billy had been released
and his mother didn't even know –
no wonder he hadn't gone back to her.

I got a taxi and asked the driver
to take me to Billy's hostel.
I had to find Billy, to see if he was all right.
The Warden was quite helpful.
Billy had been there –
he stayed for a few weeks.
Then he'd started drinking.
The hostel had to throw him out.

'Couldn't you have given him another chance?'
I said.
'He had lots of chances,' the Warden replied.
'Where did he go?' I had to find my son.
'Try one of those old houses down by the canal,'
the Warden said.
'A few lads share a squat down there.'

The Squat

It didn't take long in the taxi.
The old houses were in a mess.
Their windows were long gone –
with sheets of tin instead of glass.
The new owners were tramps and winos,
and kids who came to sniff glue.
I found one house with a light on.
I knocked and waited.
Nobody came.

The door was open, so I went inside.
A gang of kids sat on the floor.
The far-away look in their eyes
told me they were on drugs.
I had a job getting any sense out of them.
I showed them Billy's photo.
They shook their heads.
Then a girl said,
'I know him. The priest took him in. He was ill.'
'Tell me about it!' I shouted. 'It's important.'
But she didn't say any more.
She shut her eyes and lay back against the wall.
'Where can I find this priest?' I yelled.
A lad opened his eyes.
'Burton House,' he said. 'Ask for Father Paul.'

It was a mile away.
The taxi had gone.
I ran all the way.
I found Father Paul dishing up soup
to a queue of ragged old men.
He handed me a plate.
'You don't understand,' I said.
'I'm looking for Billy, my son.
For God's sake, Father, where is he?'

The Hospital

I took a bus to the hospital,
hoping and praying I wouldn't be too late –
Wilson Ward, the priest had said.
I ran along the empty corridors
looking for the right ward.
The nurses were starting to settle everyone down
for the night.
When I got to Wilson Ward
I looked along the rows of beds,
looking for Billy.
They were all old men.
Had I come to the right place?

Then I saw him –
a tall lad, well built,
bigger than I had thought he would be.
From the back I saw that his hair stuck up on end –
the way it always had.
He was wearing a white coat
and was lifting an old chap onto his bed.
I watched him smooth the pillow.
I saw the care
with which he laid the old man down.
Billy would make a fine nurse.

Then he turned round.
He knew me right away.
His face lit up in a big smile.
'Dad,' he said. 'I'm off duty in ten minutes.
Can you wait? We'll talk then.'

I could wait.
I had the rest of my life.
As I sat in the office watching Billy work
I thanked the priest with all my heart.
He'd taken Billy in
when his life had been a mess –
prison, drink and drugs.
But he'd seen something in him.
He'd been the father I should have been.
I hoped it wasn't too late to begin again.

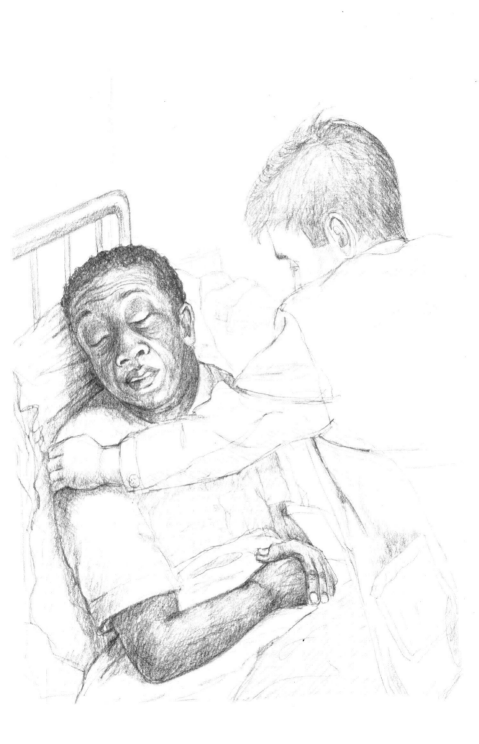